Solemn Vow

Honoring The Dogs Who Protect Us

Photographs by James Corbett

Written by James and Meaghan Corbett

DEDICATION

To the men, women, and K-9s of law enforcement. Never has there been a closer family, who has sacrificed so much, for so many.

ACKNOWLEDGMENTS

We would like to thank contributor, friend, and mentor Lansing Woo, who has always been there to provide encouragement, advice, and support. Lance is a dog's best friend and a true inspiration among the men and women of law enforcement.

We would like to thank Dr. Michael O'Brien whose editing brought great impact and value to each page; and to Gabriella Nigro for providing insightful and thoughtful improvements.

Many volunteers also helped us with designing the book, and made suggestions along the way. We thank each and everyone of you for your support and patience with Jim!

To the Rimadyl K-9 Courage Program and our Angel supporters, we thank you for your care and continued support of Police K-9s. To the Inglis Police Dog Academy and Canine Tactical Operations, we thank you for your support and contributions in helping us to better understand what it takes to become a K-9 handler.

Thank you to Vested Interest in K9s, Inc., who for the last 8 years has donated over 2400* bullet and stab protective vests, in all 50 states, to law enforcement K9s, in efforts to save the lives of these four-legged heroes. (*At the time this book went to press)

Lastly, we thank the National Police Dog Foundation and its inspiring actions and efforts to aid and assist police K-9s and their handlers nationwide. Your years of dedicated support and sacrifice have helped so many along the way.

CONTENTS

Introduction   i

1. Courageous   1

2. Vigilant   19

3. Loyal   49

4. Noble   79

5. Determined   107

6. In Remembrance   137

INTRODUCTION

Do you truly know the sheer joy of canine companionship? Do you know how it feels to be greeted day-in-and-day-out by unconditional loyalty, affection and love, which never wavers despite your ups and downs? A dog never judges, doesn't complain, just wants your attention and a playful pat or petting stroke. He is present when your kids are born, when you're sick or you're tired, and when you want to just give up; he is always there with a wagging tail just thrilled to see you and wanting most to be with you. He entertained you as a child playing in the back yard, when you came home from your first date, or graduated from high school. Perhaps he is even your most trusted companion towards the end of your life. No matter what, your dog is always there, always loyal, always devoted, and ever present just for you.

Now think of that bond and ask yourself how you would feel if on top of all of the feelings you might have for your dog, you could say your dog saved a life, perhaps YOUR life or that of someone you love. What if everyday you brought your dog to work and the two of you were able to save lives together or to find missing people dearly loved by others? What if you were able to locate and apprehend criminals who harm the ones you love, or rescue the injured, or comfort someone who lost someone they loved? How would you feel about your dog then?

Now think about losing the dog who sacrificed its life for your life or the life of someone you love, or even the life of a total stranger? How would you feel?

Over the past two years, I have had the absolute privilege of photographing a number of Police K-9s and speaking to K-9 handlers and their families. They all generously shared their stories, that include the joys, bonds and the sorrows they have faced throughout their careers. While I was only able to visit a fraction of the K-9 units throughout the country, what I observed no matter where I went was the extraordinary bond between each K-9 and its handler. It didn't have to be described or spoken about, I could just feel it. The bond between K-9 and handler was inseparable. No matter if they were young or old, new to the force or veterans, K-9 and handler were a singular force of one, joined by unconditional love, mutual respect, and most of all, the call of duty to protect and serve.

The following chapters are filled with photos and short descriptions about our nation's police K-9s who keep us safe, and of those fallen K-9s we will always be remembered, never forgotten by those they saved and those they served.

COURAGEOUS

2016 K-9 Hero of the Year, K-9 Edo saved the lives of 3 individuals, two of whom were severely wounded and being held hostage. K-9 Edo and his handler responded to the incident, which began with a car jacking, and made entry into a house where the hostage taker was holding two individuals whom he had shot. K-9 Edo bypassed the two wounded suspects, located the gunman, and took a bite-hold of the suspect's leg. K-9 Edo's response allowed sufficient time for an entry team to subdue the suspect and safely evacuate the two hostages.

K-9 Edo, Los Angeles Police Department, California

During the pursuit and apprehension of a domestic violence suspect, K-9 Sem sustained life-threatening injuries inflicted by the assailant. After making a full recovery, K-9 Sem was eager and ready to return to duty and continues to protect his fellow officers and the community of Cypress, CA.

K-9 Sem, Cypress Police Department, California

Absolutely fearless and having a strong work drive, K-9 Mojo also loves being around people. As a new team for the Metro-Nashville Police K-9 Unit, K-9 Mojo and his handler have been building a strong and unwavering bond. At a recent citizen's academy demonstration, K-9 Mojo's handler was talking with a woman who politely interrupted saying, "Officer, I believe your dog is peeing on your leg." At which time K-9 Mojo's handler looked down and responded, "Yes mam, he is."

K-9 Mojo, Metro-Nashville Police Department, Tennessee

A department veteran and recipient of the Alexandria Police Department Valor Award, K-9 Xig Xag specializes in narcotics detection, tracking, and is also a member of SWAT. By his handler's side, K-9 Xig Xag proudly serves the community of Alexandria, VA.

K-9 Xig Xag, Alexandria Police Department, Virginia

During the 2015 Labor Day weekend K-9 Boris and his handler responded to a call of a suspicious person with a possible explosive device. Ignoring the officer's commands, the suspect lunged towards a bag believed to contain an explosive device, but K-9 Boris intercepted him before he reached the bag. Upon search of the bag, no explosive was found. However, the suspect admitted he was intent upon suicide by a cop. Quick action by K-9 Boris saved the suspect's life.

K-9 Boris, Santa Monica Police Department, California

K-9 Santo is credited with saving the lives of officers on more than one occasion. Santo, who is a member of the Kenton County SWAT team, works on and off lead with members who are all able to provide K-9 Santo with commands.   In one incident a robbery suspect opened fire on investigators. K-9 Santo located the suspect hiding under a blanket and close to a hunting rifle. After the suspect refused to respond to any commands, K-9 Santo engaged the suspect and received a stab wound rendering him unconscious. As officers entered the room, K-9 Santo re-gained consciousness, and re-engaged the suspect pushing him onto his back. The suspect surrendered and officers located a loaded handgun under the blanket the suspect had over him. K-9 Santo is considered one of the most loyal and committed members of the SWAT team, but is also known for his kind and gentle demeanor, especially when surrounded by his team members' children.

K-9 Santo, Kenton County SWAT, Kentucky

As man's best friend, K-9 Yoschi enjoys spending his days at home with his handler's family. At night, K-9 Yoschi is a true hero. Facing a suspect who had ignited several cars on fire and was threatening to detonate an explosive device, K-9 Yoschi engaged the suspect, dragging him away from the burning vehicles. K-9 Yoschi's response allowed firefighters and other emergency personnel to access and gain control over the chaotic scene, while also pulling the suspect to safety.

K-9 Yoschi, Ventura County Sheriff's Office, California

A veteran from the Czech Republic, K-9 Chance has been serving the City Of Alexandria, VA since 2011. Chance is named after a "Second Chance" ballistic vest that saved his handler's life before they became partners. As talented as they come, K-9 Chance is a member of the Special Operations Team and assists on tactical operations. K-9 Chance knows only one speed whether at work or at home and that is full speed all the time!

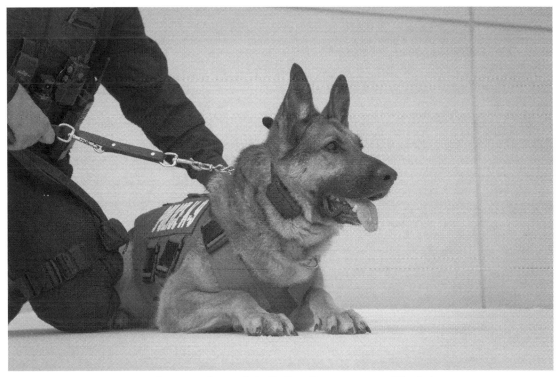

K-9 Chance, Alexandria Police Department, Virginia

18

VIGILANT

One of the oldest police K-9 Units in the country, the Topeka police K-9 Unit has a long and distinguished history of dedicated and professional service to the City of Topeka, KS. Starting with two German Shepherds in 1960, the K-9 Unit has grown and now has seven brave K-9s and handlers. Each K-9 is unique in personality and ability, but each shares the common goal of protecting and serving the citizens of Topeka.

Topeka Police K-9 Unit, Topeka Police Department, Kansas

Atascadero Police Department's newest addition K-9 Pit has displayed an extremely loyal and friendly personality, while continuing to show great drive during training and work. K-9 Pit seems happiest after a chance to bite an aggressor during training and while playing with his toy after a job well done.

K-9 Pit, Atascadero Police Department, California

As a newer addition to the Coeur d'Alene PD K-9 unit, K-9 Pecco has already facilitated numerous apprehensions, a number of which required force. In addition to his patrol work, K-9 Pecco will soon be trained in narcotics detection and will continue to capably serve the beautiful lakeside city of Coeur d'Alene.

K-9 Pecco, Coeur d'Alene Police Department, Idaho

Over the past 6 years, K-9 Rosco has been credited with the apprehension of a federal murder suspect, as well as, locating and apprehending numerous burglary, robbery and sexual assault suspects. K-9 Rosco is remarkably dedicated, versatile, and active in the Hartford community, visiting schools and performing in state wide K-9 demonstrations.

K-9 Rosco, Hartford Police Department, Connecticut

With what began as an urgent need to do more with less, in 1979 the LAPD formulated a novel program which eventually provided two K-9s the opportunity to prove their immense value in tracking dangerous suspects and being clear tactical force multipliers. Quickly and demonstratively proving its worth, the LAPD K-9 Platoon has grown considerably and is now regarded as one of the most effective and innovative K-9 units in the country.

Los Angeles Police Department K-9 Platoon, California

As an explosives detection dog for the past 5 years, K-9 Alpine has performed high priority bomb sweeps guarding United States Presidents, Secretaries of State, Senators, as well as NFL and NHL teams. With his extremely keen sense of drive and sensibility, K-9 Alpine enjoys searching vehicles on a daily basis. What disturbs him most is not being able to search every vehicle he sees, including those driving by while he sits in his handler's patrol unit.

K-9 Alpine, Metro-Nashville Police Department, Tennessee

K-9 Orbit is all business once his duty harness and collar are on him. In his 5 years of service, K-9 Orbit has been involved in approximately 50 apprehensions, several of which involved armed suspects. K-9 Orbit is highly motivated and continues to safeguard and protect Bernalillo County.

K-9 Orbit, Bernalillo County Sheriff's Department, New Mexico

On his first criminal deployment, K-9 Epic assisted a neighboring town in the search for and apprehension of an armed kidnapping and robbery suspect. As Newburyport's first and only police K-9, K-9 Epic continues to bravely serve the town and surrounding area.

K-9 Epic, Newburyport Police Department, Massachusetts

During a narcotics search of a local building, K-9 Marley located and alerted his handler to $795,990 worth of narcotics. In addition to keeping Wethersfield safe, K-9 Marley is active in local schools where he most enjoys playing with the children.

K-9 Marley, Wethersfield Police Department, Connecticut

The Las Vegas Metropolitan Police Department K-9 Unit has over 55 years of dedicated service to the City of Las Vegas. Today many of its handlers travel with 2 dogs, the first is a patrol dog and the second is an explosives detection dog. The K-9 Unit is ever-present and always working to keep the residents of Las Vegas safe and secure.

Las Vegas Metropolitan Police Department K-9 Unit, Nevada

Engaging numerous explosive sweeps, including those for the Green Bay Packers and the Wisconsin Badgers football teams, K-9 Eon has quickly become an important part of the Appleton Police Department. As soon as he hears his handler's seat belt click, K-9 Eon is up, ready, and watching his handler's back. When not working, K-9 Eon enjoys playing with his football in the backyard.

K-9 Eon, Appleton Police Department, Wisconsin

K-9 Bessi is probably one of the most social Police K-9s one will ever meet. While hard at work during a convention inside Mississippi State University's coliseum, K-9 Bessie came nose to face with a vendor's mannequin being displayed. Confused by why the mannequin wouldn't speak to her, K-9 Bessi would not leave the mannequin alone and eventually barked loudly seeking a response. Looking curiously to her handler for help, K-9 Bessie was relieved to know that mannequin wasn't a real threat or ever capable of being her friend.

K-9 Bessi, Mississippi State University Police Department, Mississippi

An expert in his field, K-9 Ringo proudly serves the state of Mississippi as an explosive detection dog. Always by his handler's side, K-9 Ringo and his handler are ever vigilant and always prepared.

K-9 Ringo, Mississippi State Fire Marshal's Office

Adopted by her handler from a local animal rescue, K-9 Zara now serves as a proud member of the Alexandria Police Department K-9 Unit. Full of energy and recent graduate of Explosive Ordinance Detection School, K-9 Zara has a new found purpose and a new best partner to help serve and protect the city of Alexandria, VA.

K-9 Zara, Alexandria Police Department, Virginia

LOYAL

K-9 Havoc's 6 years of dedicated service have included numerous criminal apprehensions and the successful location of several missing persons. In the hours and days following the Boston Marathon bombings, K-9 Havoc worked tirelessly along with regional K-9 teams and SWAT units actively searching for the bombing suspects. Today K-9 Havoc continues to provide loyal and brave service to the town of Burlington.

K-9 Havoc, Burlington Police Department, Massachusetts

Extremely loyal, K-9 Ryker assisted the Boston Police Department in the tense hours following the Boston Marathon bombing. Never more than two feet from his handler, K-9 Ryker always sits vigilantly facing the rear window of the cruiser, protectively covering his handler's back. K-9 Ryker proudly safeguards the residents of Holyoke with distinction.

K-9 Ryker, Holyoke Police Department, Massachusetts

The lone female in the K-9 unit, K-9 Shiloh, throughout her 8 years of service, has been active in narcotics enforcement and suppression efforts. Extremely loyal, she enjoys riding in the back of her handler's patrol car, watching the world go by; but to all who see her on patrol, her physical presence is a conspicuous deterrent to crime.

K-9 Shiloh, Metro-Nashville Police Department, Tennessee

On May 5, 2015, while on patrol with handler Lt. Eric Eslary, K-9 Blek sustained serious injuries in a head-on traffic collision which tragically claimed Lt. Eslary's life. After honorably serving the town of Ligonier, PA, K-9 Blek now serves as the guardian of Lt. Eslary's family.

K-9 Blek (retired), Ligonier Police Department, Pennsylvania

K-9 Buckley was an active patrol dog from 2005 to 2009 and since retirement K-9 Buckley has enjoyed the sport of dock diving and visiting local nursing homes as a registered AKC therapy dog. From 2009 to 2014, K-9 Ben worked as a patrol and narcotics detection dog, and in retirement has competed in AKC obedience and herding events. K-9 Ruffy was an explosive detection dog from 2010 to 2014, who took her job and retirement very seriously and continues to do anything for a tennis ball.

K-9 Ruffy (retired), K-9 Buckley (retired), K-9 Ben (retired), Montgomery County Police Department, Maryland

With 4 years of active service as a patrol and narcotics detection dog, K-9 Jackson has been involved in locating numerous burglary suspects. An excellent tracker, K-9 Jackson most enjoys a simple pleasure after a job well done, namely playing with his Kong toy.

K-9 Jackson, Santa Fe County Sheriff's Office, New Mexico

As a result of a bond no one could come between, K-9 Dano saved his handler's life during a life and death altercation. Without K-9 Dano's heroic intervention, an attacker would have certainly taken his handler's life. Engaging and distracting the suspect, K-9 Dano allowed his handler enough time to draw her firearm and immediately end an attack certain to have cost her life.

K-9 Dano (retired), Ventura County Sheriff's Office, California

With 7 years of service, K-9 Dusty has hundreds of deployments and over 87 arrests, including 53 felony apprehensions. While conducting an article search for a sexual assault case, K-9 Dusty picked up a different scent that led him and his handler to a woman in a drainage ditch. Had K-9 Dusty not located the woman, she would have certainly died from hypothermia. Working throughout the county, K-9 Dusty has become quite a hero to the local children, who can be heard telling their parents, "there's Dusty and that's the officer that drives him around".

K-9 Dusty, Cortez Police Department, Colorado

As a new member of the force, K-9 Wyatt patrols the streets of San Jacinto, CA. As a guardian of the city, K-9 Wyatt is an ever vigilant protector of his new home, of his new handler, and of the residents of San Jacinto.

K-9 Wyatt, Riverside County Sheriff's Department, San Jacinto Station, California

All business from the moment his duty collars are placed on him, using his ultra-sensitive nose, K-9 Murdock has successfully located missing persons by both tracking and wind scenting. K-9 Murdock has also been involved in numerous explosive detection incidents performing both protective sweeps and active threat searches. First and foremost, K-9 Murdock is a very loyal and obedient canine and a dependable and valued asset to the Sheriff's Department.

K-9 Murdock, Brown County Sheriff's Department, Green Bay, Wisconsin

With a goofy personality and loving drive, K-9 Bach is happiest when carrying his ball; until his handler leaves the room and K-9 Bach drops the ball and awaits his handlers return. Very protective, K-9 Bach fastidiously patrols the grounds of Mississippi State University as a vigilant campus guardian.

K-9 Bach, Mississippi State University Police Department, Mississippi

A retired veteran, K-9 Amigo was most happy when tracking suspects or receiving attention after showing off his abilities during local demonstrations. A loyal and vigilant partner, K-9 Amigo doesn't like his handler to be out of his sight.

K-9 Amigo (retired), Ventura Police Department, California

Dutch for buddy or partner, K-9 Makker is a truly loyal partner and companion who serves the town of East Kingston, NH. Whether deployed, or while training, he is always there for his handler, who describes him as a one in a million K-9 who never lets him down.

K-9 Makker, East Kingston Police Department, New Hampshire

Relatively new to the Alexandria Police Department, K-9 Stryker is a two and a half year old high energy German Shepherd from the Netherlands. K-9 Stryker and his handler make a truly professional team with a bond that grows stronger every day. K-9 Stryker loves his toys at home just as much as he loves them at work, jumping around like a kangaroo when wanting someone to play with him.

K-9 Stryker, Alexandria Police Department, Virginia

NOBLE

In remembrance and in honor of those who have fallen, K-9 Shiloh stands watch over the National Law Enforcement Officers Memorial in Washington, DC. K-9 Shiloh and her handler patrol the grounds of the national monuments as guardians, protectors, and constant reminders of the sacrifices our law enforcement and military heroes have made.

K-9 Shiloh, United States Park Police, Washington, DC

Like his namesake on the hit show Law and Order, K-9 Lenny Briscoe has a nose for crime and over four years of tracking experience. While tracking and locating an elderly patient who wandered away from a senior care facility in cold weather conditions. K-9 Briscoe successfully tracked through thick woods and safely located the individual who was treated for minor injuries. As a former show dog, K-9 Briscoe is most happy performing for an audience and gleefully starts baying whenever an audience begins to clap during K-9 demonstrations.

K-9 Lenny Briscoe, Columbia Police Department, South Carolina

Credited with over 23 felony apprehensions in his five years of service, K-9 Aris can be fierce when on the job, K-9 Aris, but displays a friendly and gentle disposition when interacting with the pubic. A career-ending injury forced the Cypress Police Department to retire K-9 Aris in 2013, and in retirement Aris enjoys his days in New Mexico as a police K-9 goodwill ambassador.

K-9 Aris (retired), Cypress Police Department, California

On Thanksgiving 2015, K-9 Luke apprehended an armed suicidal female who had placed herself and numerous innocent by-standers in extreme danger. K-9 Luke's apprehension saved the suspect's life and avoided a use of deadly force situation.

K-9 Luke, Boise Police Department, Idaho

Sometimes stubborn, but always accurate, K-9 Roscoe has made a name for himself with the number of lost and missing people he has safely rescued. K-9 Roscoe remains forever dedicated to finding those who are lost, from the young to the old.

K-9 Roscoe, Los Angeles County Sheriff's Department, California

Another ambassador for Police K-9s is Yeti. While Yeti hasn't apprehended any criminals or saved any lives, she is the proud mom of many offspring K-9s who have. Overseeing some of her sons and even grandsons, Yeti spends much of her time watching over the K-9 training fields as a proud mom.

Police K-9 mom Yeti, California

Over her 8 years of service K-9 Ziva has worked to socialize newly acquired K-9s. She has been an active Police K-9 ambassador with the public; and being very social and non-dominant, she helps newly acquired dominant alpha males to relax and interact without aggression. Ziva sets a very high standard in obedience and obstacle course mastery for new K-9s to emulate. When not training, Ziva enjoys being around horses and working cattle.

Police K-9 Ambassador Ziva, National Police Dog Foundation, California

A rescue dog who was brought in from the "streets" and trained for duty, K-9 Oakley now serves as the newest addition to the city of Ludlow as a narcotics detection dog. While K-9 Oakley enjoys narcotics detection work, his main passion is tracking and perhaps one day K-9 Oakley will find a lost soul or missing person, just as someone found him.

K-9 Oakley, Ludlow Police Department, Kentucky

Rich with history, the city of Kingman, Arizona is protected and served by K-9 Cirus. New to the force, Cirus and his veteran handler now capably patrol the streets of Kingman, which include the heart of historic Route 66.

K-9 Cirus, Kingman Police Department, Arizona

K-9 Migel absolutely loves his job protecting the students and faculty at Mississippi State University. It is likely K-9 Migel's ulterior motive for loving his job is being rewarded with his ball which he loves to play with after a job well-done. So much so, he lays on his back with his ball in his mouth, then with his two paws, tosses his ball across the room. K-9 Migel's handler can't recall ever seeing another dog who enjoys playing fetch with himself.

K-9 Migel, Mississippi State University Police Department, Mississippi

Often spotted patrolling Albuquerque's late night events and major festivals, K-9 Kyra diligently works to protect the city and residents as an explosive detection dog. When you will most likely not see K-9 Kyra is in the early morning, as Kyra absolutely loves sleeping in!

K-9 Kyra, Albuquerque Police Department, New Mexico

While still new to the force, K-9 Yankee and his partner endured some really rough incidents while apprehending the toughest of criminals. It was during these most trying times that K-9 Yankee and his partner forged an inseparable bond of trust, respect, and absolute loyalty. Years later, the two still patrol the streets of Ventura as partners, always there for each other and keeping Ventura residents safe.

K-9 Yankee, Ventura Police Department, California

A certified veteran, K-9 Odin is a certified Patrol, Narcotics Detection and Tracking K-9. While at work and at home, K-9 Odin loves to play fetch with his tug toys. While on the job with the Alexandria Police Department, K-9 Odin especially enjoys finding hidden narcotics and playing hide and seek with the bad guys.

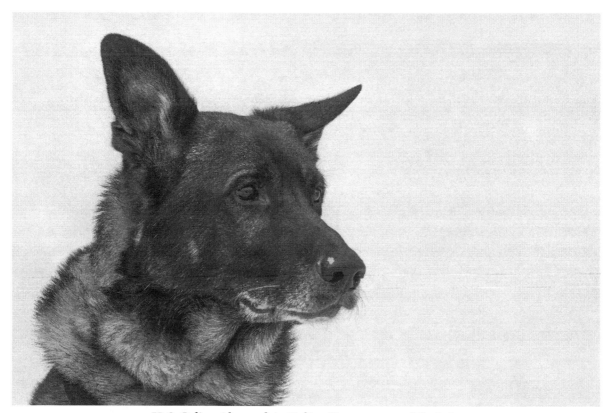

K-9 Odin, Alexandria Police Department, Virginia

DETERMINED

K-9 Jett assisted the Hartford SWAT team in the search for and apprehension of a convicted felon who fired multiple rounds during an attempted car jacking. K-9 Jett has received multiple awards for his ongoing assistance with narcotic investigations and apprehensions in the city of West Hartford and surrounding areas.

K-9 Jett, West Hartford Police Department, Connecticut

During the search for an armed homicide suspect, K-9 Diesel successfully alerted to his handler the suspect's location in an area unsafe for his handler and fellow officers to enter. K-9 Diesel was released and after an ensuing struggle, the suspect was successfully apprehended and his weapon located.

K-9 Diesel, Boise Police Department, Idaho

K-9 Brando and his handler were involved in a vehicle pursuit of three armed robbery suspects. When the suspects abandoned their stolen vehicle, K-9 Brando tracked the suspects and located them in a wooded area. The suspects, one of whom was still armed with a handgun, were safely taken into custody and were recently sentenced to 16-22 years in prison.

K-9 Brando, Greensboro Police Department, North Carolina

Over the past 4 years, K-9 Ringo has demonstrated strong motivation and work performance, which is balanced by a fun-loving personality. A new team for the Metro-Nashville Police Department, K-9 Ringo and his handler each day face new learning opportunities and obstacles which clearly strengthen the bond of trust between the two.

K-9 Ringo, Metro-Nashville Police Department, Tennessee

An elderly person who was suffering from a self-inflicted wound, could not be found after wandering into an isolated wooded area. Deployed to find the individual, K-9 Ellie Mae quickly did what first responders could not. Soon after identifying the scent from the individual's vehicle, K-9 Ellie Mae located the elderly person who lay on the ground and was incoherent. First responders rendered first aid and transported the individual to the emergency room, thus saving a life.

K-9 Ellie Mae, Greensboro Police Department, North Carolina

During the Fall of 2014, K-9 Jax tracked and located a 2 year old girl who had been missing for almost 24 hours in a heavily wooded area. The rescued child was happily reunited with her family, and today K-9 Jax continues to protect the citizens of the state of Michigan.

K-9 Jax, Michigan State Police

As an active drug and patrol dog for the past 6 years, K-9 Drager has consistently been involved in the major drug seizures in the state of Vermont. K-9 Drager has been named Vermont Drug Dog of the Year for the past 4 years and is known for his unique and quirky counter-clockwise search direction. Having a mind of his own, in a two door office, K-9 Dragger will only go in one and out the other.

K-9 Drager, Vermont State Police

While en route in response to a bank robbery, K-9 Gero and his handler located the suspect walking down the street. When the suspect refused to respond to commands, K-9 Gero was released and apprehended the suspect. The suspect assaulted both Gero and his handler, but was eventually restrained and subdued and taken into custody. K-9 Gero continues to bravely serve and protect the city of Greensboro.

K-9 Gero, Greensboro Police Department, North Carolina

Prior to joining the Bernalillo County Sheriff's Department, K-9 Xar was a patrol dog in Geneva, Switzerland. K-9 Xar is an exceptional tracker, holding the rare ability to track off lead. K-9 Xar is extremely social and enjoys being mixed into a large search team as well as working with the SWAT team.

K-9 Xar, Bernalillo County Sheriff's Department, New Mexico

K-9 Cletus has excelled at facilitating numerous felony apprehensions, the first of which was the tracking and apprehension of an aggravated burglary suspect. He is known in the K-9 section by his nickname of "Tigger" as he loves to jump for toys or anything that looks remotely interesting. When not working and catching felons, K-9 Cletus loves to chase leaves and dutifully collecting them in his mouth during break time.

K-9 Cletus, Metro-Nashville Police Department, Tennessee

Referred to as a "wolf" by local school children, K-9 Blaze is an extremely devoted and determined dog. When a suspect in a police pursuit crashed his car and fled the scene, but left a large amount of cash behind, K-9 Blaze tracked off the scent on the money and located the suspect as well as some concealed narcotics. narcotics. K-9 Blaze continues to protect and valiantly serve the city of New Britain.

K-9 Blaze, New Britain Police Department, Connecticut

Though on the job for only four months, K-9 Lex has already gained respect as a reliable and essential addition to the Wisconsin Rapids Police Department. Always excited to go "on duty," K-9 Lex is a quick learner and has been involved in numerous deployments to protect and serve the residents of Wisconsin Rapids.

K-9 Lex, Wisconsin Rapids Police Department, Wisconsin

Described by his handler as having a nose like a vacuum cleaner, K-9 Carlo loves tracking suspects and has aided in the arrest and capture of numerous armed and dangerous felons. During one pursuit involving armed robbery suspects throwing firearms from their vehicle, K-9 Carlo and his handler intervened and stopped four suspects dead in their tracks. One look at K-9 Carlo, and apparently no one dare tried running away. While not tracking dangerous felons, K-9 Carlo is as friendly as they come.

K-9 Carlo, Greensboro Police Department, North Carolina

New to the Alexandria Police Department, K-9 Zeus recently completed K-9 Basic Patrol School. With graduation in sight, K-9 Zeus and his partner will soon complete Explosive Ordinance Detection School and will be out on the streets.

K-9 Zeus, Alexandria Police Department, Virginia

IN REMEMBRANCE

We dedicate the In Remembrance chapter to those K-9s who died in the line of duty, and to the handlers who have endured the loss of a partner. A dog is a man's best friend; a Police K-9, is a partner, a friend, and a life that will never be forgotten.

2015 FALLEN K-9s

1. K-9 Blue, Georgetown County Sheriff's Office, South Carolina, EOW 1/10/2015
2. K-9 Sultan, Riverside County Sheriff's Office, California, EOW 1/21/2015
3. K-9 Pepper, Wise County Sheriff's Office, Texas, EOW 1/28/2015
4. K-9 Mako, Cleveland County Sheriff's Office, North Carolina, EOW 2/19/2015
5. K-9 Fritzie, Bath Police Department, West Virginia, EOW 3/12/2015
6. K-9 Barney, Tacoma Police Department, Washington, EOW 3/25/2015
7. K-9 Harry, Audubon County Sheriff's Office, Iowa, EOW 3/28/2015
8. K-9 Bella, Maryland Division of Correction, EOW 4/15/2015
9. K-9 Jimmy, King County Sheriff's Office, Washington, EOW 4/18/2015
10. K-9 Igor, Kissimmee Police Department, Florida, EOW 4/21/2015
11. K-9 Hector, Hialeah Police Department, Florida, EOW 5/27/2015
12. K-9 Jimmy, Hialeah Police Department, Florida, EOW 5/27/2015
13. K-9 Chewbacca, Hancock County Sheriff's Office, Mississippi, EOW 6/15/2015
14. K-9 Nitro, Stockton Police Department, California, EOW 6/30/2015
15. K-9 Baston, Savannah State University Police Department, Geogria, EOW 7/10/2015
16. K-9 Titus, Little Rock Police Department, Arkansas, EOW 7/15/2015
17. K-9 Zane, Conyers Police Department, Georgia, EOW 7/16/2015
18. K-9 Zeke, Muldrow Police Department, Oklahoma, EOW 7/23/2015
19. K-9 Jola, Jim Wells County Sheriff's Office, Texas, EOW 8/10/2015
20. K-9 Falko, Toledo Police Department, Ohio, EOW 8/12/2015
21. K-9 Wix, Brown County Sheriff's Office, Wisconsin, EOW 8/12/2015
22. K-9 Dingo, Maryland Division of Correction, EOW 8/25/2015
23. K-9 Kojack, Maryland Division of Correction, EOW 8/25/2015
24. K-9 Ike, Vancouver Police Department, Washington, EOW 9/2/2015
25. K-9 Dutch, Minneapolis Police Department, Minnesota, EOW 9/5/2015
26. K-9 Koa, Lander Police Department, Wyoming, EOW 10/16/2015
27. K-9 Hyco, Anderson County Sheriff's Office, South Carolina, EOW 10/21/2015

2016 FALLEN K-9s

1. K-9 Jojo, San Bernardino County Sheriff's Department, California, EOW 1/06/2016
2. K-9 Jethro, Canton Police Department, Ohio, EOW 1/10/2016
3. K-9 Krijger, Norfolk Police Department, Virginia, EOW 1/11/2016
4. K-9 Ogar, Smith County Constable's Office, Texas, EOW 1/19/2016
5. K-9 Jag, Twin Rivers Unified School District Police Department, California, EOW 1/20/2016
6. K-9 Kobus, Omaha Police Department, Nebraska, EOW 1/23/2016
7. K-9 Betcha, Rutland County Sheriff's Office, Vermont, EOW 1/29/2016
8. K-9 Aren, Port Authority, Allegheny County Police Department, Pennsylvania, EOW 1/31/2016
9. K-9 Vigor, Monroe County Sheriff's Office, Tennessee, EOW 3/09/2016
10. K-9 Reefer, Chelan County Sheriff's Office, Washington, EOW 3/09/2016
11. K-9 Nicky, Las Vegas Metropolitan Police Department, Nevada, EOW 3/31/2016
12. K-9 Aldo, Unified Police Department of Greater Salt Lake City, Utah, EOW 4/27/2016
13. K-9 Bruno, Anaheim Police Department, California, EOW 5/18/2016
14. K-9 Suki, Westchester County Department of Public Safety, New York, EOW 5/20/2016
15. K-9 Ledger, La Salle County Sheriff's Office, Texas, EOW 5/29/2016
16. K-9 Duke, Richland Parish Sheriff's Office, Louisiana, EOW 6/01/2016
17. K-9 Rex, San Juan Police Department, Texas, EOW 6/02/2016
18. K-9 Inca, Cherokee County School District Police Department, Georgia, EOW 6/10/2016
19. K-9 Bruno, Amarillo Police Department, Texas, EOW 6/12/2016
20. K-9 Lazer, United States Department of Homeland Security, CBP, Texas, EOW 6/20/2016
21. K-9 Tyson Fountain County Sheriff's Office, Indiana, EOW 6/27/2016
22. K-9 Credo, Long Beach Police Department, California, EOW 6/28/2016
23. K-9 Roscoe, Emmett police Department, Idaho, EOW 7/01/2016
24. K-9 Totti, Pennsylvania Department of Corrections, Pennsylvania, EOW 7/07/2016
25. K-9 Mojo, Arlington Police Department, Texas, EOW 7/19/2016
26. K-9 Bak, Stephens County Sheriff's Office, Oklahoma, EOW 8/04/2016
27. K-9 Amigo, Kingman Police Department, Arizona, EOW 8/20/2016

2016 FALLEN K-9s

28. K-9 Ty Vom Friedrichsfelder Eck, California City Police Department, California, EOW 9/07/2016
29. K-9 Lina, Madison County Sheriff's Office, Arkansas, EOW 9/09/2016
30. K-9 Helo, Alaska State Troopers, Alaska, EOW 9/25/2016
31. K-9 Jardo, Boise Police Department, Idaho, EOW 11/16/2016
32. K-9 Thor, Wethersfield Police Department, Connecticut, EOW 11/22/2016
33. K-9 Payne, Pembroke Police Department, North Carolina, EOW 11/29/2016

*Information on Fallen K-9s obtained from Officer Down Memorial Page (odmp.org), as well as individual law enforcement officers and organizations.

On June 24, 2013, K-9 Kilo confronted an armed subject who had barricaded himself in a neighboring home. Using courageous action, K-9 Kilo was mortally wounded while locating the subject, but saved the lives of the on scene responding officers. K-9 Kilo sacrificed his life to keep the human officers safe. Rest in peace K-9 Kilo.

K-9 Kilo, Indiana State Police-EOW 6/24/2013

By the age of 4 months, K-9 Adam was trained to find heroin, methamphetamines, cocaine, and marijuana and by 6 months of age was already on drug duty in the jail. As dedicated and persistent adversaries, inmates would create distractions with "meows" from their cells, all to no avail, only amusing K-9 Adam. Small in stature, K-9 Adam had a huge personality, always loving to be around anyone trying to pet him, poke his ears or even pull his tail. Thank you for your dedicated service. Rest in peace K-9 Adam.

K-9 Adam (retired), Santa Barbara County Sheriff's Office-Custody Division/Classification Unit, California-EOW 6/15/15

Photo provided by: Tracey Martinez

K-9 Kody was an 8-year veteran of the St. Paul Police Department K-9 Unit, who, on February 12, 2012, with his handler, assisted the US Marshals Federal Fugitive Task Force in the search for a child molestation and rape suspect. When K-9 Kody assisted officers in locating the suspect in a basement, the suspect refused to comply with commands, and K-9 Kody deployed and bit the suspect's forearm. During the ensuing struggle, the suspect, armed with a knife, stabbed K-9 Kody twice near the chest. Despite aggressive resuscitation attempts, K-9 Kody succumbed to his injuries. K-9 Kody's heroic efforts saved the lives of the officers in the room, who themselves would have been stabbed trying to apprehend the suspect. Rest in peace K-9 Kody.

K-9 Kody, St. Paul Police Department, Minnesota-EOW 2/12/2012
Photo provided by: Brad Smith

In the early morning of October 7, 2013, Edmonton Police Officers responded to a call of a possibly armed man near a convenience store. The suspect refused to comply with officer commands and led the officers in a dangerous high-speed pursuit. When the suspect exited his vehicle and attempted to escape, K-9 Quanto immediately pursued and apprehended the suspect. As K-9 Quanto bit the suspect, the suspect drew a knife and stabbed K-9 Quanto multiple times in the chest. K-9 Quanto succumbed to his injuries at the scene. K-9 Quanto's truly heroic actions and sacrifice allowed his handler and fellow officers to apprehend the suspect without injury to themselves. Rest in peace K-9 Quanto.

K-9 Quanto, Edmonton Police Department, Canada-EOW 10/7/2013
Photo provided by: Brad Smith

On December 30, 2009, K-9 Rocky saved the lives of numerous SWAT officers and Sheriffs deputies when he was deployed into the house of a barricaded suspect. The suspect had fired shots on officers who were assisting a female in the process of recovering a vehicle from the suspect's property. In the ensuing 15-hour stand off, K-9 Rocky was deployed ahead of the SWAT unit and located the suspect, who mortally wounded K-9 Rocky. The suspect then attempted to engage the SWAT team, who mortally wounded the suspect. K-9 Rocky will be forever remembered for courageously protecting his fellow officers. Rest in peace K-9 Rocky.

K-9 Rocky, Anoka County Sheriff's Department, Minnesota-EOW 12/30/2009
Photo provided by: Brad Smith

On January 30, 2013, K-9 Koda and his handler responded to an anonymous call regarding the location of a shooting suspect. The suspect refused to comply with officer commends and lead the officer on a high-speed pursuit. When the suspect attempted to escape after exiting his vehicle, K-9 Koda immediately pursued. As K-9 Koda jumped to bite the suspect, the suspect fired a single shot to K-9 Koda's upper back. Although mortally wounded, K-9 Koda bravely and tenaciously continued biting to subdue the suspect, allowing his handler and fellow officers time to safely apprehend the suspect. Rest in peace K-9 Koda.

K-9 Koda, Leon County Sheriff's Department, Florida-EOW 1/30/2013
Photo provided by: Brad Smith

Following his nose and doing what he did best, K-9 Sultan tracked a fleeing felon into a crawlspace underneath a house. K-9 Sultan, in pursuit of the individual was shot in the neck by the suspect, later dying in route to the hospital. K-9 Sultan will be remembered as a loyal and courageous K-9 hero, but will be most remembered by his partner, his handler, and his best friend. Rest in peace K-9 Sultan.

K-9 Sultan, Riverside County Sheriff's Office, California-EOW 1/21/2015
Photo provided by: Freddie B Photography.

Caught off guard by a hail of forty rounds of gunfire, K-9 Kezno moved between his handler, partner, and an armed murder suspect. Advancing towards the threat and drawing gunfire, K-9 Kenzo sustained two gunshot wounds that barely missed vital organs. After a full recovery, K-9 Kenzo returned to duty and continued to serve the county of Palm Beach, Florida. Kenzo received the Medal of Honor for saving the lives of his handler and partner by allowing them sufficient time to respond to the threat. In his retirement, K-9 Kenzo enjoyed his walks in a nearby park and spending time with his handler. K-9 Kenzo passed away in 2016. Rest in peace K-9 Kenzo.

K-9 Kenzo, Palm Beach County Sheriff's Office, Florida-EOW 2016

ABOUT THE AUTHOR/PHOTOGRAPHER

Jim Corbett is a career law enforcement officer, whose off-duty passion is animal photography specializing in photography for non-profit animal rescue and working dog organizations. While not taking photographs, Jim and his wife/veterinarian Meaghan, volunteer their time assisting working dog organizations with veterinary care. Together, Jim and Meaghan find great joy and personal satisfaction in sharing time with working dogs and their handlers and providing veterinary and volunteer support. They are ably assisted and supported by their own dogs, Cooper and Kayla, who enjoy spending their time chasing chipmunks.

VESTED INTEREST IN K9s, INC.

Of the 34 K9s killed in the line of duty in 2016, 15 possibly might have been prevented with a bullet and stab protective vest, just like the ones Vested Interest in K9s, Inc. is committed to providing to the over 30,000 law enforcement dogs in the United States. Since 2009, more than 2,400 law enforcement K9s, in all 50 states, including some of the K9s mentioned in this book, have received a vest from Vested Interest in K9s, Inc.

They Protect Us.

We Protect Them.

The K9s in this book vested by VIK9s are as follows:
K9 PIT, ATASCARDERO PD, CA
K9 ROSCO, HARTFORD PD, CT
K9 BORIS, LAS VEGAS METROPOLITAN PD, NV
K9 BLEK, LIGONIER PD, PA
K9 RYKER, HOLYOKE PD, MA
K9 OAKLEY, LUDLOW PD, KY
K9 JETT, WEST HARTFORD PD, CT
K9 DRAGER, VERMONT STATE PD
K-9 MAKKER, EAST KINGSTON PD, NH
K-9 STRYKER, ALEXANDRIA PD, VA
K-9 ZARA, ALEXANDRIA PD, VA
K-9 XIG XAG, ALEXANDRIA PD, VA
K-9 CHANCE, ALEXANDRIA PD, VA
K-9 ODIN, ALEXANDRIA PD, VA
K-9 ZEUS, ALEXANDRIA PD, VA

Follow Us:

508-824-6978

RIMADYL®
K★9 COURAGE
PROGRAM
Supporting K-9s who served us.

Our Angel supporters thank the men and women of law enforcement for their service to their communities and encourage you to support you local Police K-9 units as well as your local working dog and animal rescue organizations.

Made in the USA
San Bernardino, CA
30 April 2017